TANKFUL OF THANKFUL!

Tankful of Thankful!
with Maximilian

Written by Jeannie Lee Eddy
and Adrian Meyer Mallin

XULON PRESS

Dedication:
For every child with a thankful heart,
this is for YOU!

Special thankfulness to
Dylan and Braydon Leslie for their
creative input and awesome ideas!

And special thanks to Tim Clark for
weaving this joy between
Jeannie Lee Eddy and Adrian Meyer Mallin!

Xulon Press
2301 Lucien Way #415
Maitland, FL 32751
407.339.4217
www.xulonpress.com

© 2018 by Jeannie Lee Eddy and Adrian Meyer Mallin
Art by ChrisPadovano

Printed in the United States of America.

www.littlechildrensbooks.com
facebook.com/littlechildrensbooks

ISBN-13: 9781545630792

Maximilian was getting dressed for his first day of Kindergarten! Maxi came into the kitchen and his Mommy told him that breakfast was ready.

"WOW, my favorite breakfast," exclaimed Maxi. "You made me Happy Face pancakes!!" "Yes," replied mommy. "It s a special day and I am so thankful that you are starting school!"

With a mouthful of pancakes, Maxi asked,
"What does *thankful* mean?"

"It means you are happy and give thanks for what you have." said Mommy.
"It looks like YOU have a MOUTHFUL OF THANKFUL Maxi."

"Now, let's think of everything that makes us thankful," said Mommy, "because we always want to be thankful!!"

After finishing all of his pancakes,
Maximilian said, "My belly is full, so I
have a BELLYFUL OF THANKFUL! "

"Yes, you are so smart." said Mommy,
"Here is your lunch bag and yes,
you now have a BAGFUL OF THANKFUL!"

Mommy then remembered that today
is show and tell. Mommy asked Maxi,
"What do you want to bring?"
"What about my sand bucket full of
sea shells?" Maxi responded
"That's a BUCKETFUL OF THANKFUL!!"

Maximilian thought some more and
exclaimed, "I love my doggie Sebastian,
I love my family, and I love all of my toys!"

Well then, we have a HOUSEFUL OF
THANKFUL", said mommy

Just as Mommy handed Maximilian his backpack, Maxi shouted, "Mommy, I have a BACKPACKFUL OF THANKFUL!! "
"Yes you do!" replied Mommy.

They arrived at school and as Mommy brought Maxi into his classroom, his eyes lit up with amazement! There were so many interesting things to see on the walls, on the tables, and all over the room!

Mommy introduced Maxi to his
teacher, Mrs. Leslie.
"Maxi, we are so happy to have you
here with us" said Mrs. Leslie.
"You will make many new friends
and learn many new things!"

Maxi leaned over and said to his Mommy,
"I have a SCHOOLFUL OF THANKFUL!"
"Yes you do" replied Mommy!

Then Mrs. Leslie took the children outside
to play and Maxi ran to his favorite
part of the playground, the swings!

As he jumped on the closest one
and began to swing, he exclaimed,
"Now I have a SWINGFUL OF THANKFUL!"

When the bell rang, school was over and
Maxi walked out to greet his mommy
who was waiting to pick him up
and take him home.

Maxi gave his Mommy a great big hug!
While Mommy was asking Maxi about
his first day at school, she noticed that
they had to head to the gas station
on the way home because the
fuel gauge was on empty!

They arrived at the gas station,
and after filling the tank up with gas,
Maxi exclaimed, "MOMMY, now we have a
TANKFUL OF THANKFUL!!!!"

Meet the Authors

Jeannie Lee Eddy is an Ordained Minister, Published Author, Educator, and Speaker working in ministry and writing Little Children's Books to share the love of God around the world. She holds a Master's Degree and serves on the board of Directors with several Ministries. She is a proud Mommy and Grand Mommy and lives in Florida near her children.

Adrian Meyer Mallin has led an accomplished life filled with travel ,dancing, and mothering. She was born in Roslyn, NY, and schooled at The George Washington University. She has lived her life loving most importantly, her two sons, Ross and Andrew Mallin. As a business owner, she was featured on The Today Show and has always planned to succeed in as many pursuits as possible. She has an exuberant desire to travel the world, see different cultures and dance on every continent. She has authored one previous book Mother Love Now and After I'm Gone - TANKFUL OF THANKFUL is her first children's book.

Printed in the USA
CPSIA information can be obtained
at www.ICGtesting.com
LVHW010155131023
760667LV00008B/31